MACROS COOKBOOK 2021

Weight Lose with the Macro Diet and Burn your Fat!

TABLE OF CONTENT

INTRODUCTION

What is a macro?

There are three macronutrients in every bite of food you eat: protein, carbohydrates, and fat. While many foods contain all of these macronutrients, most are heavily targeted towards one or two of them. For example, meat is loaded with protein, bread is mostly made up of carbohydrates, and olive oil is mostly fat. Your body needs all three functions to function.

According to the macro diet, you can lose weight by setting a goal for how many grams of protein, carbohydrates, and fat you eat per day. Unlike most traditional diets, you don't need to count calories, and unlike low-carb or low-fat diets, you don't need to remove your favorite foods like potatoes, pasta, or bacon. In theory, the IIFYM plan allows you to eat anything you want, as long as it fits your macro count.

What are macronutrients, and how do you calculate how much you need?

A lot is written about macronutrients on this blog. That is not without reason: they form the basis of your diet and have a considerable influence on your body's functioning. Yet, it may well be that you slowly get lost a bit when it comes to those macros. What exactly are they, and what do they all do?

And above all: what role should they play in your diet? Today we put all that information clearly under each other. After reading this blog post, you will know exactly what you get from which macronutrients - and how much you want to eat!

What are Macronutrients?

Macronutrients are, in short, the nutrients or nutrients that provide energy to the body. So your body needs them for practically everything you do, be it active sports or just regulating your metabolism. In general, we distinguish three important macros: proteins, carbohydrates, and fats.

Alcohol is sometimes referred to as the fourth macronutrient because it also supplies calories to your body. However, alcohol has no necessary role and is therefore not a 'mandatory' part of your diet. Therefore, we will leave the fourth macro in the rest of this blog aside for a moment.

Below are the three important macronutrients.

1. Proteins

Proteins are simply the building blocks of your body. They consist of amino acids, creating muscle and other tissue types. Because your body is constantly being renewed, you need them constantly! Proteins contain four calories per gram.

You will find them primarily in animal products: meat, fish, poultry, dairy, and eggs. Also, there are vegetable proteins: legumes, grains, nuts, and soy, for example. The disadvantage of vegetable proteins is that they do not contain all amino acids. However, you still get everything you need by combining it with different types.

2. Carbohydrates

Carbohydrates are your body's primary energy providers. This makes them more efficient than fats, for example, more difficult to convert. Like proteins, they provide four calories per gram.

There are many carbohydrate-rich products, but it is best to choose slow carbohydrates. The glucose is absorbed more slowly. That way, there will be no spike in your blood sugar! Good carbohydrates include whole grains, oatmeal, and semi- grains such as quinoa, buckwheat, and amaranth. Also, vegetables and certain fruits are good sources of carbohydrates.

3. Fats

Fats are often seen as 'unnecessary,' but they are not! For example, you need fats to build cells. Fat is also important for absorbing many nutrients, such as the fat-soluble vitamins A, D, and E. Fat is more energy-rich than the other two macronutrients, at nine calories per gram.

Again, it is important to distinguish between healthy and unhealthy fats. It is better to avoid processed trans fats. Healthy options include fatty fish, nuts, avocado, olives, and olive oil. Animal fats are also fine to a limited extent.

Macronutrient ratio

Because all macros have different functions, it matters in what proportion you eat them. There is no single perfect rule of thumb. The number of macronutrients you need mainly depends on the physical goals you set for yourself. Do you mainly want to lose weight, or are you trying to build muscle?

In the first case, you need fewer carbohydrates because you first want to get enough fats and proteins. Only then fill up the remainder with carbohydrates. If you want to build muscle, you will eat more carbohydrates in proportion. After all, you have to eat more, which leaves more room for calories from carbohydrates after those proteins and fats.

Calculate macronutrients

Calculating your macronutrients is done in three steps:

How Much Protein Do You Need? For strength athletes, that's about 1.8 grams per kilogram of body weight, so Albert eats 144 grams of protein per day. Those who exercise less actively can also go for 1 to 1.5 grams.

How many fats do you need? The rule of thumb here is about 1 gram per kilo of body weight. Albert, therefore, eats about 80 grams of fat per day.

How many carbohydrates can you still eat? Albert eats 144 x 4 = 576 calories of protein, and 80 x 9 = 720 calories of fat. Since he wants to eat 3,000 calories, he has 1704 calories left for carbohydrates. That is 1704/4 = 426 grams of carbohydrates per day.

When you eat fewer calories in total, you will also 'have' fewer carbohydrates. Therefore, a diet with which you lose weight is relatively often lower in carbohydrates!

Counting calories?

Crucial in the macronutrient ratio is the total number of calories you eat. Even the perfect ratio between nutrients is not effective if you consume too many or too few calories on a structural basis. Based on your goals, try to create a surplus or deficit anywhere from 300-500 calories using the above ratios as a guideline.

Whether you want to count calories constantly is completely up to you. If you don't feel like constantly keeping track of what you eat, it is wise to do it for a few weeks. This gives you a good insight into your diet and how much you consume.

MACRO DIET RECIPES

Stuffed tomatoes with couscous, sheep cheese and zucchini

Ingredients For 4 persons

- 75 g Instant couscous
- salt
- 4 (approx. 1 kg) Ox heart tomatoes
- 1 (approx. 180 g) small zucchini
- 2 Red onions
- 1 tbsp olive oil
- 1 pinch sugar
- 1/2 tsp dried oregano
- pepper
- 75 g Feta cheese
- 150 ml Vegetable broth

preparation

30 minutes

1. Put the couscous in a large bowl. Pour 75 ml of boiling salted water over it and let it steep for about 5 minutes. Fluff with a fork and let cool

2. In the meantime, wash the tomatoes. Cut about 1/5 of the tomato as a "lid" at the base of the stem. Hollow out tomatoes. Cut the inside of the tomato (approx. 100 g) into small pieces. Wash and clean the zucchini and cut into small cubes. Peel and halve the onions and cut into fine pieces

3. Heat oil in a pan. Fry the onions and zucchini for 3-4 minutes. Just before the end of the cooking time, add the chopped tomato pulp. Season with salt, sugar, oregano and pepper. Crumble the feta with your hands. Add the zucchini mixture and feta to the couscous and mix in

4. Place the tomatoes in an ovenproof baking dish, season the couscous mixture again with salt and pepper and fill the tomatoes. Either put the lid on the tomatoes or just put them in the baking dish. Pour in the stock and cook in the preheated oven (electric stove: 200 ° C / convection: 175 ° C / gas: see manufacturer) for about 15 minutes

Macros Nutritional info

1-person approx:

- 190 kcal790 kJ
- 9 g protein
- 7 g fat
- 23 g of carbohydrates

Upper core vital crackers

Ingredients For 40 pieces

- 200 g Whole grain rice
- Salt pepper
- 200 g colorful quiona
- 40 g sesame
- 50 g linseed
- 40 g Chia seeds
- 40 g Sunflower seeds
- Parchment paper

preparation

180 minutes

1. Bring rice, 1 teaspoon salt and 800 ml water to the boil. Cook uncovered over low to medium heat for about 35 minutes. Rinse the quinoa in a sieve and cook the rice for about 15 minutes. Then take the saucepan off the stove and let stand covered for about 10 minutes.
2. Preheat the oven (electric stove: 180 ° C / convection: 160 ° C / gas: see manufacturer). Add the sesame, linseed, chia seeds, sunflower seeds and 1⁄4 teaspoon pepper to the rice mix and stir in with a wooden spoon. Quarter the dough, roll out one after the other on a piece of baking paper as thinly as possible and cut into approx. 10 pieces each.
3. Pull one after the other onto a baking sheet and bake in the hot oven on the bottom shelf for about 30 minutes. Let cool down. In addition, z. B. Avocado Cream and Pea Sprouts.

Macros Nutritional info

1-piece approx:

- 60 kcal
- 2 g protein
- 2 g of fat
- 7 g of carbohydrates

Fitness salad with hazelnut dressing

Ingredients For 4 persons

- 2 tbsp ground hazelnut kernels
- 250 g Mushrooms
- 1 clove of garlic
- 4 tbsp oil
- salt
- pepper
- 1 (approx. 250 g) Fennel bulb
- 1 red pepper
- 1/2 Head of oak leaf lettuce
- 100 g Rocket
- 3 tbsp light balsamic vinegar
- sugar
- 25 g Sprout mix

preparation

20 minutes

1. Roast the hazelnuts in a pan without fat for 1–2 minutes, remove and let cool
2. Trim, clean and halve the mushrooms. Peel the garlic and cut into fine pieces. Heat 1 tablespoon of oil in a pan. Fry the mushrooms for about 5 minutes while turning. After 1–2 minutes add the garlic and fry with it. Season the mushrooms with salt and pepper

and remove from the pan

3. Clean, wash and thinly slice the fennel. Clean and wash the peppers and cut into small cubes. Pluck oak leaf lettuce into bite-sized pieces, wash thoroughly and drain in a colander. Wash rocket thoroughly, cut off the stems and drain well. Mix together the roasted hazelnuts and vinegar, season with salt, pepper and sugar. Gradually beat in 3 tablespoons of oil

4. Put the sprouts in a colander, rinse with cold water and drain. Mix the lettuce, bell pepper, mushrooms, fennel and dressing and arrange on 4 plates. Garnish with sprouts. Baguette bread tastes good with it

Macros Nutritional info

1-person approx:

- 180 kcal750 kJ
- 6 g protein
- 15 g fat
- 6 g of carbohydrates

Scrambled eggs with spring onions on whole meal bread

Ingredients For 1 person

- 2 handle (s) Parsley and dill
- 1 Spring onion
- 1 tomato
- 1 Egg (size M)
- salt
- 1 slice Whole grain bread
- pepper
- oil

preparation

10 mins

1. Wash the herbs, shake dry, pluck the leaves from the stems and chop. Clean and wash the spring onions and cut into rings except for something to garnish. Wash and clean tomatoes, cut 2 slices and dice remaining tomatoes. Whisk the egg and herbs. Season with salt

2. Brush a coated pan with oil and heat. Briefly fry the spring onion rings and diced tomatoes in a hot pan. Season with salt. Add the egg and bring to a stop while stirring

3. Arrange bread, tomato slices and scrambled eggs on a plate. Garnish with spring onions. Season with pepper

Macros Nutritional info

1-person approx:

- 190 kcal790 kJ
- 12 g protein
- 7 g fat
- 20 g of carbohydrates

Zucchini noodles with prawns

Ingredients For 4 persons

- 500 g frozen raw shrimp (headless, in shell)
- 2 yellow and green zucchinis (approx. 300 g each)

- 2 Garlic cloves
- 2 Organic lemons
- salt
- pepper
- 1 tbsp oil
- 4 stem (s) parsley

preparation

20 minutes

1. Put the prawns in a colander and let thaw for about 1 hour. Peel the prawns, remove the intestines, wash and pat dry. Wash zucchini, rub dry and peel into strips with a julienne peeler.
2. Peel and finely dice the garlic. Wash 1 lemon and rub dry. Rip off the shell. Halve the lemon and squeeze out the juice. Wash the parsley, shake dry and pluck the leaves from the stems.
3. Season the prawns with salt and pepper, heat the oil in a pan. Fry the prawns in it, turning, for about 5 minutes. Remove and add zucchini noodles to the pan. Fry for about 2 minutes, turning, season with salt and pepper.
4. Add the prawns, lemon zest and juice, simmer for about 2 minutes. Wash the rest of the lemon, rub dry and cut into thin wedges. Mix the parsley into the zucchini noodles and serve.
5. Garnish with lemon wedges.

Macros Nutritional info

1-person approx:

- 160 kcal670 kJ
- 23 g protein
- 5 g of fat
- 6 g of carbohydrates

Vegetable soup (basic recipe)

Ingredients For 4 persons

- 1 Vegetable onion
- 400 g Potatoes
- 400 g Carrots
- 200 g tomatoes
- 200 g Celery (with leafy green)
- 2 Garlic cloves
- 1 tsp black peppercorns
- 1 Clove
- 1 Juniper berry
- 1 Bay leaf
- 3 tbsp butter
- 1.5 l Vegetable broth
- Salt pepper
- grated nutmeg
- fresh herbs

preparation

45 minutes

1. Peel and halve the onion and cut into strips or small cubes. Peel and wash the potatoes. Peel the carrots. Cut the potatoes and carrots into small cubes. Wash, clean, quarter and

cut tomatoes.

2. Clean and wash the celery and cut into approx. 0.5 cm thin slices. Set aside some green leaves from the celery. Peel garlic and chop finely.
3. Put the peppercorns, clove, juniper berries and bay leaf in a tea bag.
4. Heat the butter in a large saucepan. Steam the onions and garlic until translucent. Add the finely chopped vegetables and sauté for 1-2 minutes.
5. Pour in the vegetable stock, add the tea bag with the spices and a large pinch of salt. Bring the soup to the boil and simmer for about 15 minutes.
6. Season the soup with salt, pepper and nutmeg. Garnish with leafy greens from the celery and fresh herbs and serve.

Macros Nutritional info

1 portion approx:

- 213 kcal
- 5 g protein
- 7 g fat
- 29 g of carbohydrates

Fried eggs on spinach

Ingredients For 4 persons

- 1 onion
- 1 clove of garlic
- 2-3 tbsp butter
- 1 kg Frozen spinach leaves
- Salt pepper
- nutmeg
- 4th Eggs

preparation

40 minutes

1. Peel and finely chop the onion and garlic. Heat the butter in a large saucepan. Sauté the onion and garlic until translucent. Add the frozen spinach and approx. 150 ml water and bring to the boil. Cover and let thaw over low heat for about 15 minutes.
2. Stirring occasionally.
3. Drain the spinach, squeeze out lightly. Season with salt, pepper and nutmeg and divide into four small or one large casserole dish. Beat 1 egg on each. In the preheated oven (electric stove: 225 ° C / convection: 200 ° C / gas: see p.
4. Manufacturer) let stand for about 10 minutes. Season with salt and pepper. Cheese crostini also taste great.

Macros Nutritional info

1-person approx:

- 180 kcal
- 14 g protein
- 12 g fat
- 2 g of carbohydrates

STUFFED PEPPERS WITH TURKEY

Ingredients For 1 person

- 75 g Turkey schnitzel
- 1/2 (155 g) Bag of ready-made sauerkraut
- 1 Stalk parsley
- 2 tbsp low-fat yoghurt
- 1/2 tsp hot mustard
- salt
- pepper
- 1/2 red pepper
- 1 tsp oil
- Sweet paprika

preparation

15 minutes

1. Wash the meat, pat dry and cut into cubes. Put the sauerkraut in a sieve, rinse briefly under cold water and allow to drain. Wash the parsley, pat dry and cut the leaves into strips.
2. Mix the yoghurt and mustard and season with salt and pepper. Clean and wash the peppers. Heat oil in a pan. Fry the peppers all around for 1-2 minutes, then keep warm. Put the turkey cubes in the hot pan, fry for 2-3 minutes and season with salt, pepper and paprika powder.

3. Add the sauerkraut and heat for about 3 minutes. Pour the turkey meat and sauerkraut into the warm half of the pepper and pour the mustard cream on top. Sprinkle with parsley strips and a little paprika powder.

Macros Nutritional info

1-person approx:

- 190 kcal790 kJ
- 23 g protein
- 8 g of fat
- 6 g of carbohydrates

Quick carrot soup with chicken

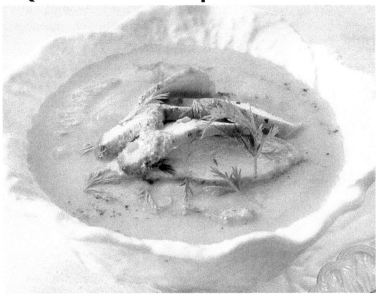

Ingredients For 4 persons

- 750 g Bunch of carrots
- 150 g Potatoes
- 2 Onions
- 2 tbsp olive oil
- 1 tbsp Vegetable broth (instant)
- salt

- pepper
- nutmeg
- Sweet paprika
- 2 Chicken fillets (approx. 150 g each)
- 4 tsp green pesto (glass)

preparation

25 minutes

1. Clean the carrots, wash some greens. Peel, wash and slice carrots. Peel, wash and dice the potatoes. Peel and dice the onions. Heat 1 tablespoon of oil in a saucepan. Sauté onions, potatoes and carrots in it. Pour in 1 liter of hot water, stir in the stock. Season with salt, pepper and nutmeg. Simmer for about 15 minutes.
2. In the meantime, wash the chicken and pat dry. Season with salt, pepper and paprika. Fry in 1 tablespoon of hot oil for about 10 minutes.
3. Puree the soup and season to taste. Chop the carrot greens. Cut the meat into slices. Serve with the carrot greens and pesto on the soup. Bread tastes good with it.

Macros Nutritional info

1 portion approx:

- 160 kcal
- 13 g protein
- 6 g fat
- 13 g of carbohydrates

Fried asparagus salad with strawberries

Ingredients For 4 persons

- 2 kg white asparagus
- 250 g Strawberries
- 2-3 tbsp oil
- 75 g powdered sugar
- 100 ml Balsamic vinegar
- salt
- coarse black pepper from the mill
- 2 bunches (approx. 200 g) arugula

preparation

50 minutes

simple

1. Wash and peel the asparagus and cut off the woody ends generously. First halve the asparagus stalks lengthways, then cut into 3–5 cm long pieces. Wash and clean the strawberries and cut in half or into quarters depending on the size.
2. Heat oil in a large pan. Fry the asparagus in it for 2-3 minutes. Dust with icing sugar and caramelize briefly while turning. Deglaze with vinegar and 100 ml water, bring to the boil and simmer over low heat for 6–8 minutes.

3. Season to taste with salt and pepper. Fold in the strawberries. Take everything out of the pan and let cool down a bit.
4. Clean and wash the rocket, spin dry and, if necessary, pluck it smaller. Lift under the asparagus salad and serve. Fresh baguette tastes good with it.

Macros Nutritional info

1-person approx:

- 200 kcal
- 8 g protein
- 5 g of fat
- 30 g of carbohydrates

Mediterranean tomato soup

Ingredients For 4 persons

- 2 Spring onions
- 1 clove of garlic
- 3 tbsp olive oil
- 1 tbsp Tomato paste
- 500 ml Vegetable broth
- 1 can (s) (425 ml) tomatoes
- salt
- pepper
- Sweet paprika
- sugar
- 1/2 425- ml can of small white bean kernels
- 1 (approx. 200 g) small zucchini
- 75 g Cherry tomatoes
- 7 stem (s) thyme

preparation

30 minutes

1. Wash and clean the spring onions. Cut the green and white parts into rings separately. Peel and roughly chop the garlic. Heat 1 tablespoon of oil in a saucepan. Sauté the light spring onion rings and garlic for 2-3 minutes, then stir in the tomato paste. Sauté the tomato paste for 1–2 minutes, deglaze with the stock and tomatoes. Season with salt, pepper, paprika and a little sugar, cover and simmer for about 20 minutes

2. Pour beans into a colander and rinse under cold water. Wash and clean the zucchini, halve lengthways and cut into slices. Wash and quarter the tomatoes. Heat 2 tablespoons of oil in a pan. Fry the zucchini in it, turning, for about 5 minutes until light brown. Add tomatoes, beans and green spring onion rings and fry for approx. 1 minute. Season the vegetables with salt and pepper, set aside

3. Wash the thyme, shake dry and finely chop the leaves of 3 stems. Add the chopped thyme to the soup, puree and season to taste. Arrange the soup in bowls and distribute the vegetables in the middle. Garnish with the remaining thyme and serve immediately

Macros Nutritional info

1-person approx:

- 180 kcal750 kJ
- 7 g protein
- 8 g of fat
- 15 g of carbohydrates

Fiery shrimp pan

Ingredients For 4 persons

- 400 g frozen, raw shrimp (without head and shell)
- 3 zucchinis
- 1 federal government Spring onions
- 300 g Cherry tomatoes
- 5 Garlic cloves
- 3 Chili peppers
- 1 federal government parsley
- 3 tbsp olive oil
- salt
- pepper

preparation

20 minutes

1. Place the shrimp in a colander and rinse with cold water. Put on a plate and let thaw. Wash and clean the zucchini, halve lengthways and cut into large pieces. Clean and wash the spring onions and cut into fine rings.
2. Wash tomatoes. Peel the garlic and cut in half lengthways. Clean the chilli peppers, cut lengthways, wash and remove the seeds. Cut the chilli peppers into fine strips. Wash the parsley, pat dry and finely chop.

3. Rinse the prawns in cold water, drain on kitchen paper. Heat 2 tablespoons of oil in a pan. Fry the prawns vigorously for 2–3 minutes, turning, remove and place on a plate.
4. Add 1 tablespoon of oil to the frying fat. Fry the spring onions and zucchini in it, turning. Add the cherry tomatoes, garlic and chili peppers. Add the prawns again, season with salt and pepper. Sprinkle with parsley.

Macros Nutritional info

1-person approx:

- 190 kcal790 kJ
- 22 g protein
- 7 g fat
- 10 g of carbohydrates

Tomato curry soup with goat cream cheese

Ingredients For 4 persons

- 1 onion
- 1 clove of garlic
- 3 tbsp olive oil
- 1 tbsp Tomato paste
- 1 tbsp Flour
- 2 tbsp Curry powder
- 1 can (s) (850 ml) tomatoes
- 400 ml Vegetable broth
- 1 untreated lemon
- 6 stem (s) thyme
- salt
- pepper
- 1-2 tbsp honey
- 100 g Goat cream cheese

preparation

35 minutes

1. Peel the onion and garlic and cut into fine cubes. Heat 1 tablespoon of oil. Sauté the onion and garlic in it for about 3 minutes while stirring. Add tomato paste, flour and curry and sauté briefly.

2. Add tomatoes and broth, bring to the boil and simmer for about 15 minutes, stirring occasionally. Wash lemon with hot water, rub dry. Peel off the shell in thin strips with a zest. Halve the fruit and squeeze out the juice.
3. Wash the thyme, shake dry, pluck the leaves from the stems. Finely chop the lemon zest and thyme, place in a bowl and mix with 1–2 tablespoons lemon juice and 2 tablespoons oil. Season with salt and pepper.
4. Finely puree the soup with a hand blender and season with salt, pepper and honey. Crumble the cheese over the soup and add some gremolata.

Macros Nutritional info

1-person approx.:

- 180 kcal750 kJ
- 5 g protein
- 10 g fat
- 16 g of carbohydrates

Stuffed peppers with spinach and egg

Ingredients For 4 persons

- 4th red peppers
- 4th Shallots
- 2 Garlic cloves
- 250 g Cherry tomatoes
- 300 g Spinach leaves
- 4 stems flat leaf parsley
- 1 Organic lemon
- 1 tbsp oil
- salt
- pepper
- sugar
- 4th Eggs (size M)

preparation

75 minutes

1. Wash the peppers and cut off the end of the stem as a lid. Remove cores.
2. Peel and finely dice shallots and garlic. Wash tomatoes. Sort the spinach, wash and drain well. Wash parsley and shake dry, pluck the leaves, chop. Wash the lemon with hot water, dry it and finely grate the peel. Halve the lemon and squeeze one half.
3. Heat the oil in a saucepan, fry the shallots and garlic in it for about 1 minute. Add tomatoes, lemon zest and juice. Cover and simmer over medium heat for about 5

minutes. Add the spinach, parsley and 5 tablespoons of water. Season with salt, pepper and sugar, simmer for about 3 minutes.

4. Preheat the oven (electric stove: 200 ° C / convection: 175 ° C / gas: see manufacturer). Place the peppers in a baking dish and fill with the spinach mixture. Cook in the hot oven for about 45 minutes. After approx. 15 minutes, break open 1 egg and slide into each pod. Then put on the pepper lids.

5. Remove the paprika, season the eggs with salt and pepper. If you don't pay too much attention to carbohydrates, mashed potatoes will taste great with it.

Macros Nutritional info

1 portion approx:

- 180 kcal
- 13 g protein
- 10 g fat
- 13 g of carbohydrates

Fennel salad with tuna

Ingredients For 4 persons

- 3 tomatoes
- 2 Fennel bulbs
- Juice of 1 lemon
- 1 (approx. 300 g) small cucumber
- 3 Garlic cloves
- 1 federal government coriander
- salt
- pepper
- 2 tbsp olive oil
- 2 can (s) (185 g each) Tuna in its own juice

preparation

30 minutes

1. Wash, clean, core and cut tomatoes into pieces. Wash and clean the fennel and cut into fine strips. Put both in a bowl and drizzle with lemon juice
2. Peel the cucumber and cut off the ends. Core and dice the cucumber. Peel and chop the garlic. Wash the coriander, shake dry, pluck the leaves and cut into strips. Put everything in the bowl. Season with salt and pepper and pour in the oil. Mix everything
3. Drain the tuna and cut into large pieces. Spread on the salad just before serving

Macros Nutritional info

1-person approx.:

- 170 kcal710 kJ
- 21 g protein
- 6 g fat
- 6 g of carbohydrates

Vegetarian stir-fry vegetables with eggs

Ingredients For 4 persons

- 1 onion
- 2 Garlic cloves
- 1 tbsp oil
- 1 (480 g) Bag of frozen vegetables "Balkan Art"
- 1 can (s) (425 ml) tomatoes
- 1-2 tbsp Harissa paste
- 1/2 tsp ground cumin
- salt
- 1 pinch sugar
- pepper

- 4th Eggs (size M)

preparation

25 minutes

1. Peel onions and garlic and cut into small pieces. Heat the oil in an ovenproof pan. Sauté the onion and garlic for 2-3 minutes while turning. Add the frozen vegetables and 2 tablespoons of water, bring to the boil and simmer for about 2 minutes.
2. Add tomatoes, harissa and cumin and simmer for another 4–5 minutes. Season to taste with salt, sugar and pepper.
3. Beat the eggs and let them slide carefully into the pan. Let stand in the preheated oven (electric stove: 175 ° C / convection: 150 ° C / gas: see manufacturer) for about 10 minutes. Baguette bread tastes good with it.

Macros Nutritional info

1-person approx.:

- 200 kcal840 kJ
- 11 g protein
- 12 g fat
- 10 g of carbohydrates

Chicken skewer on a colorful garden salad with a herb and sour cream dressing

Ingredients For 4 persons

- 1/2 small cucumber
- 1 Head of kohlrabi
- 200 g Baby romaine lettuce
- 4–6 stem (s) mixed herbs (e.g., parsley, chervil, dill, basil)
- 100 g lactose-free sour cream
- 4-5 tbsp lactose-free milk
- salt
- pepper
- Lemon juice
- sugar
- 1 (approx. 200 g) Chicken fillet
- Sweet paprika
- 2 tbsp oil
- 1/2 glass pickled corncobs
- 8th Wooden skewers

preparation

20 minutes

1. Wash and clean the cucumber. Peel the kohlrabi. Thinly slice or slice the cucumber and kohlrabi. Clean, wash and cut the lettuce. Wash the herbs, shake dry and chop the leaves.

2. Mix together sour cream, chopped herbs and milk. Season the dressing with salt, pepper, lemon juice and a little sugar. Wash the chicken fillet, pat dry and cut into slices / strips. Place the chicken strips in waves on 8 wooden skewers and season with salt, pepper and a little paprika.

3. Heat the oil in a pan and fry the skewers in 2 portions for 3-4 minutes while turning. Pour off the corncobs and let them drain. Mix the cucumber, kohlrabi, corn on the cob and lettuce. Arrange the chicken skewers on the salad and drizzle with the dressing.

Macros Nutritional info

1-person approx:

- 200 kcal840 kJ
- 14 g protein
- 14 g fat
- 5 g of carbohydrates

Cauliflower with breadcrumbs

Ingredients For 4 persons

- Head of cauliflower (approx. 1 kg)
- 3-4 tbsp vinegar
- salt
- 75 ml milk
- discs toast
- 5 tbsp butter

preparation

40 minutes

1. Remove the green bracts from the cabbage. Place the cauliflower upside down in 2-3 liters of cold water with vinegar for approx. 10 minutes to remove any insects that may be present.
2. If the cauliflower is cooked whole, shorten the stalk up to the roots of the first florets and cut crosswise - it has the same cooking time as the florets. Wash cabbage.
3. For cauliflower florets, cut or break off the florets one at a time from the stalk with a small knife. Pluck off small leaflets that are still attached to the lower florets. Wash the florets.
4. Put the cabbage in a saucepan and pour in water until everything is covered. Add about 1 teaspoon of salt. Pour in milk, this will keep the cauliflower nice and white. Bring to a boil. Cover the florets and cook for 6–8 minutes, the whole head for 18–20 minutes.
5. Crumble the toast with your hands. Toast until golden brown in a pan without fat. Add butter, melt in it. Spread the crumbly butter over the cauliflower.

Macros Nutritional info

1-person approx.:

- 160 kcal
- g protein
- 11 g fat
- 10 g of carbohydrates

Asian curry chicken soup

Ingredients For 4 persons

- 3 Chicken fillets (approx. 400 g)
- 1 onion
- 1/2 Lemongrass stalk
- 1 piece (s) (approx. 1 cm, 5–10 g) ginger
- 1 small red chili pepper
- 1 Bay leaf
- black peppercorns
- salt
- 2 red pepper
- 300 g White cabbage
- 1/2 bunch coriander
- 1 can (s) (228 ml) Bamboo shoots in slices
- 50 g Bean sprouts (mung bean sprouts)

preparation

60 minutes

1   Wash the chicken fillets and pat dry. Halve the onion. Place the onion halves in a pan with the cut surface facing down and roast them until they are dark brown. Flatten the lemongrass.

2 Peel the ginger and cut into thin slices. Halve the chilli, remove the seeds and cut into small pieces. Bring the chicken fillets and 1.5 liters of cold water to the boil and season with bay leaf, ginger, lemongrass, peppercorns, chilli, onion halves and salt.

3 Let the broth simmer over medium heat for 30–40 minutes. Halve the paprika, clean and wash. Cut the bell pepper into strips. Clean and wash the white cabbage and cut into strips. Remove the meat, let it cool down a bit and cut into cubes.

4 Wash the coriander, shake dry and put 4 stalks aside. Pluck the remaining leaves from the stems and chop them into small pieces. Strain the stock through a strainer or a very fine sieve. Cook the white cabbage in the chicken stock for 10–15 minutes, season with curry and salt.

5 Add paprika and bamboo strips after about 5 minutes. Finally add the sprouts, cubed chicken and coriander, bring to the boil. Arrange in bowls and garnish with coriander.

Macros Nutritional info

1-person approx:

- 140 kcal580 kJ
- 25 g protein
- 1 g fat
- 6 g of carbohydrates

Spelled apple muesli with yogurt

Ingredients For 1 person

- 50 g Spelled flakes
- 1/2 tsp Sesame seeds
- 1/2 Apple
- 1 tsp Sultanas
- 1 tbsp low-fat yoghurt
- 1 tsp honey

preparation

15 minutes

1 Roast the spelled flakes and sesame seeds in a pan without fat, turning for about 5 minutes, remove. Quarter the apple, remove the core and dice the pulp, except for a thin apple slice for decoration.

2 Add the sultanas and apple cubes to the pan. Pour 4 tablespoons of water and allow to soak in the closed pan for about 5 minutes. Let cool down. Arrange the muesli and yoghurt in a bowl, drizzle with honey and decorate with apple slices.

Macros Nutritional info

- 1-person approx:
- 270 kcal1130 kJ
- 8 g protein
- 3 g of fat

- 52 g of carbohydrates

Scrambled eggs with spring onions on whole meal bread

Ingredients For 1 person

- handle (s) Parsley and dill
- 1 Spring onion
- 1 tomato
- 1 Egg (size M)
- salt
- 1 slice Whole grain bread
- pepper
- oil

preparation

10 mins

1   Wash the herbs, shake dry, pluck the leaves from the stems and chop. Clean and wash the spring onions and cut into rings except for something to garnish. Wash and clean tomatoes, cut 2 slices and dice remaining tomatoes. Whisk the egg and herbs. Season with salt

2   Brush a coated pan with oil and heat. Briefly fry the spring onion rings and diced tomatoes in a hot pan. Season with salt. Add the egg and bring to a stop while stirring

3   Arrange bread, tomato slices and scrambled eggs on a plate. Garnish with spring onions. Season with pepper

Macros Nutritional info

1-person approx.:

- 190 kcal790 kJ
- 12 g protein
- 7 g fat
- 20 g of carbohydrates

Papaya with grainy cream cheese

Ingredients For 1 person

- 100 g papaya
- 200 g grained cream cheese
- handle (s) Lemon balm
- 1 tsp Mineral water
- 1 tsp Lemon juice

preparation

10 mins

1 Remove the seeds from the papaya. Peel the pulp and cut into cubes. Mix the papaya and cream cheese. Wash lemon balm, pat dry, pluck leaves from 1 stalk and roughly chop.
2 Stir the leaves, mineral water and lemon juice into the cream cheese, arrange and decorate with the rest of the lemon balm.

Macros Nutritional info

1-person approx.:

- 220 kcal920 kJ
- 27 g protein
- 9 g fat
- 6 g of carbohydrates

Breakfast smoothie with berries, spinach and mango

Ingredients For 4 persons

- 50 g Baby spinach leaves
- 1 (approx. 400 g) Split pineapple
- 1/2 (approx. 300 g) mango
- 150 g Blueberries
- 125 g Raspberries
- 500 ml Buttermilk
- 4 tsp linseed

preparation

15 minutes

1 Wash and drain the spinach. Clean the pineapple, cut 8 nice slices to decorate. Peel the remaining pineapple and cut into small pieces. Cut the mango pulp from the stone and peel. Pick the berries. Set aside some raspberries to decorate
2 Finely puree the fruits, spinach and buttermilk and pour into glasses. Place the flax seeds on top, decorate with raspberries and pineapple slices. Serve immediately

Macros Nutritional info

1 glass approx:

- 160 kcal670 kJ
- 7 g protein
- 3 g of fat
- 22 g of carbohydrate

Whole grain bread with quark, banana slices, agave syrup and chia seeds

Ingredients For 4 persons

- 2 tbsp lowfat quark
- 3 tsp Chia seeds
- salt
- 2 tsp Agave syrup
- 1 Splash of lime juice
- 1 (approx. 160 g) banana
- slices Whole grain bread (approx. 45 g each)

preparation

10 mins

1 Mix the quark with chia seeds, except for something to garnish, and season with salt, 1 teaspoon agave syrup and lime juice. Peel and slice the banana.
2 Spread the quark on bread, cover with banana like tiles, sprinkle with chia seeds and drizzle with agave syrup.

Macros Nutritional info

1-person approx:

- 150 kcal630 kJ
- 8 g protein
- 1 g fat
- 27 g of carbohydrates

Fruit salad

Ingredients For 4 persons

- Kiwi fruit (approx. 300 g)
- 1/4 (approx. 400 g) pineapple
- 1 (approx. 400 g) mango
- 1 (approx. 200 g) orange
- 1 (approx. 200 g) Grapefruit
- 1 (approx. 500 g) pomegranate
- 75 g Physalis
- 1 (approx. 150 g) banana

- (approx. 400 g) Apples
- 25 g Walnut kernels

preparation

20 minutes

1   Peel the kiwis, quarter them lengthways and cut into slices. Peel the pineapple, remove the stalk and cut into pieces. Cut the mango from the stone. Peel the pulp, cut into thin wedges, cut the wedges in half.

2   Peel the orange and grapefruit so that the white skin is completely removed. Remove the fillets with a sharp knife from between the separating skins. Squeeze the juice out of the separating membranes, collect it. Halve the pomegranate horizontally, knock the seeds out of the peel with a spoon.

3   Remove the physalis from the shell, wash and cut in half if necessary. Peel and slice the banana. Wash the apples, rub dry, cut eighths and remove the core. Cut eighths into slices.

4   If necessary, halve the nut halves and mix with the fruit and juice. Arrange the fruit salad in bowls.

Macros Nutritional info

1-person approx:

- 290 kcal1210 kJ
- 4 g protein
- 6 g fat
- 52 g of carbohydrates

Millet porridge with figs

Ingredients For 2 persons

- 120 g millet
- 350 ml Almond drink
- 1 packet Bourbon vanilla sugar
- 1/2 tsp cinnamon
- sea-salt
- 8th Figs
- 4 tbsp Chia seeds

preparation

25 minutes

1   Rinse millet thoroughly under hot water. Bring the almond drink, vanilla sugar, cinnamon and salt to the boil in a saucepan, cover and simmer gently for 5–7 minutes on the lowest setting. Let the porridge swell for about 10 minutes.
2   Wash figs and cut into wedges. Spread the porridge in bowls, spread the figs on top and sprinkle with chia seeds.

Macros Nutritional info

1 portion approx:

- 230 kcal960 kJ
- 6 g protein
- 4 g of fat
- 38 g of carbohydrates

Whole grain bread with avocado and pomegranate seeds

Ingredients For 4 persons

- 1/2 pomegranate
- 1 (200 g each) Mug of grainy cream cheese
- 1 (approx. 300 g) avocado
- slices Whole grain bread (approx. 45 g each)
- Chilli flakes

preparation

15 minutes

1   Halve the pomegranate and knock out the seeds with a spoon. Halve the avocado, remove the stone, remove the pulp from the skin and cut into wedges.

2   Brush the bread slices with cream cheese, place the avocado on top like a roof tile and sprinkle with pomegranate seeds and chilli flakes.

Macros Nutritional info

1-person approx:

- 270 kcal1130 kJ
- 11 g protein
- 16 g fat
- 22 g of carbohydrates

Rye rolls with cheese, radishes and sprouts

Ingredients For 1 person

- sheets green salad (e.g., endive)
- radishes
- 1 Rye rolls (approx. 80 g each)
- 1/2 tbsp (15 g) lowfat quark
- 1 slice (30 g) reduced-fat Gouda cheese (17% fat)
- 10 g Alfalfa sprouts

preparation

5 minutes

Wash and pluck the lettuce. Clean and wash the radishes and cut into thin slices. Cut the bread rolls. Brush the lower half with quark. Halve the cheese slice. Cover the rolls with lettuce and cheese.

Sprinkle with sprouts and radishes and place the top half of the bun on top.

Macros Nutritional info

1-person approx.:

- 300 kcal1260 kJ
- 18 g protein
- 6 g fat
- 41 g of carbohydrates

Braised aubergines and peppers with ginger sauce

Ingredients For 4 persons

- Eggplant (approx. 250 g each)
- 2 red peppers (approx. 200 g each)
- 1 green pepper
- 2 tbsp olive oil

- Garlic cloves
- 50 g Ginger tuber
- 2 tbsp Soy sauce
- 1 tbsp Rice vinegar
- 3–4 stem (s) coriander
- 20 g Sesame seeds

preparation

25 minutes

1. Wash the aubergine, rub dry, cut in half lengthways and cut into pieces. Halve the peppers, clean, wash and cut into strips. Heat the oil in a large pan, fry the aubergines until golden, add the paprika.
2. Braise the vegetables for about 10 minutes while turning.
3. Peel and chop garlic and ginger, add to vegetables, deglaze with soy sauce and vinegar.
4. Wash the coriander, pat dry and finely chop. Roast the sesame seeds in a pan until golden, remove. Pour the sesame seeds and coriander over the vegetables.

Macros Nutritional info

1-person approx:

- 160 kcal670 kJ
- 5 g protein
- 11 g fat
- 8 g of carbohydrates

Asian curry chicken soup

Ingredients For 4 persons

- Chicken fillets (approx. 400 g)
- 1 onion
- 1/2 Lemongrass stalk
- 1 piece (s) (approx. 1 cm, 5–10 g) ginger
- 1 small red chili pepper
- 1 Bay leaf
- black peppercorns
- salt
- red pepper
- 300 g White cabbage
- 1/2 bunch coriander
- 1 can (s) (228 ml) Bamboo shoots in slices
- 50 g Bean sprouts (mung bean sprouts)

preparation

60 minutes

1. Wash the chicken fillets and pat dry. Halve the onion. Place the onion halves in a pan with the cut surface facing down and roast them until they are dark brown. Flatten the lemongrass.
2. Peel the ginger and cut into thin slices. Halve the chilli, remove the seeds and cut into small pieces. Bring the chicken fillets and 1.5 liters of cold water to the boil and season with bay leaf, ginger, lemongrass, peppercorns, chilli, onion halves and salt.

3   Let the broth simmer over medium heat for 30–40 minutes. Halve the paprika, clean and wash. Cut the bell pepper into strips. Clean and wash the white cabbage and cut into strips. Remove the meat, let it cool down a bit and cut into cubes.

4   Wash the coriander, shake dry and put 4 stalks aside. Pluck the remaining leaves from the stems and chop them into small pieces. Strain the stock through a strainer or a very fine sieve. Cook the white cabbage in the chicken stock for 10–15 minutes, season with curry and salt.

5   Add paprika and bamboo strips after about 5 minutes. Finally add the sprouts, cubed chicken and coriander, bring to the boil. Arrange in bowls and garnish with coriander.

Macros Nutritional info

1-person approx:

- 140 kcal580 kJ
- 25 g protein
- 1 g fat
- 6 g of carbohydrates

Bean counter pot plus turbo tofu

Ingredients For 4 persons

- 200 g Baby spinach
- Onions
- 1 piece (approx. 2 cm) ginger
- 1 red chilli pepper
- 400 g tofu
- Salt, pepper, garam masala
- 1/2 tsp cumin
- 2-3 tbsp food starch
- 2 tbsp oil
- 400 g Frozen peas

preparation

30 minutes

1 Sort the spinach, wash and shake dry. Peel and finely dice the onions and ginger. Clean the chilli pepper, cut lengthways, core, wash and cut into rings.

2 Cut the tofu into approx. 2 cm cubes. Season with 1 teaspoon each of salt and pepper, toss in the cornstarch. Heat the oil in a large saucepan. Fry the tofu all around until golden brown and remove.

3 Sauté the onion, ginger and chilli in the hot frying fat. Sprinkle with 1–2 teaspoons Garam Masala and 1⁄2 teaspoon each of salt and cumin, sweat briefly. Add 1⁄8 l water and frozen peas, bring to the boil. Cook for 2-3 minutes. Fold in the spinach and let it

collapse. Add the tofu and reheat briefly. Rice goes well with it.

Macros Nutritional info

1 portion approx:

- 290 kcal
- 24 g protein
- 11 g fat
- 22 g of carbohydrates

Stuffed zucchini with ricotta and ham

Ingredients For 4 persons

- discs White bread from the previous day
- 150 ml milk
- 4th small zucchini (approx. 150 g each)
- handle (s) basil
- 1/2 bunch parsley
- Garlic cloves

- discs cooked ham (approx. 30 g each)
- 125 g Ricotta cheese
- 1 Egg (size M)
- 2 tbsp oil
- salt
- pepper
- fat

preparation

45 minutes

1 Soak the bread in milk for about 15 minutes. Clean and wash the zucchini, cut off the upper third lengthways. Carefully hollow out the zucchini. Chop the pulp. Wash the herbs, shake dry, pluck the leaves off and cut into small pieces. Peel garlic and chop finely. Cut ham into strips.

2 Lightly squeeze out the bread, mix with the ricotta, egg, 2 tablespoons of oil, 3/4 of the herbs, garlic, zucchini pulp and strips of ham, season with salt and pepper.

3 Fill the hollowed-out zucchini with the mixture, place in a greased baking dish. Drizzle with 1 tablespoon of oil and bake in the preheated oven (electric stove: 175 ° C / fan: 150 ° C / gas: level 2) for about 25 minutes. Remove the zucchini, arrange and sprinkle with the remaining herbs.

Macros Nutritional info

1-person approx:

- 230 kcal960 kJ
- 12 g protein
- 16 g fat
- 12 g of carbohydrates

Topless teriyaki schnitzel

Ingredients For 4 persons

- 500 g broccoli
- 300 g Carrots
- Spring onions
- 1 clove of garlic
- 1 piece Ginger (approx. 1 cm)
- 6th thin turkey schnitzel (approx. 100 g each)
- 4 tbsp sesame
- 3 tbsp oil
- 5-6 tbsp Teriyaki sauce
- Salt pepper
- spice powder

preparation

40 minutes

1. Clean and wash broccoli and cut into small florets. Peel and wash the carrots, halve lengthways and cut diagonally into thin slices. Clean and wash the spring onions and cut diagonally into rings approx. 1 cm thick. Peel and finely chop the garlic and ginger. Wash the schnitzel, pat dry and cut in half crosswise.

2. Roast the sesame seeds in a large pan without fat and remove. Heat 2 tablespoons of oil in the pan. Fry the broccoli and carrots in it for 4–5 minutes. Add the spring onion rings and fry for about 1 minute. Deglaze with 2 tablespoons of teriyaki sauce and season

with salt, pepper and 5-spice powder.

3   Meanwhile season the meat with salt and pepper. Heat 2 tablespoons of oil in a second large pan. Fry the schnitzel in portions over high heat for about 1 minute on each side. Remove the finished schnitzel. Briefly sauté the garlic and ginger in the frying fat. Deglaze with the remaining teriyaki sauce and turn the schnitzel in it. Serve with vegetables and sesame seeds.

Macros Nutritional info

1 portion approx:

- 350 kcal
- 42 g protein
- 14 g fat
- 12 g of carbohydrates

Fabulous honey chicken in coconut curry

Ingredients For 4 persons

- Chicken breasts (with skin, on bone; approx. 450 g each)
- Salt, coarse pepper, curry powder, ground cumin
- 3 tbsp oil
- 1 tbsp yellow curry paste
- 1 can (s) (400 ml each) unsweetened coconut milk
- 1 lime
- 2 tbsp Liquid honey
- 500 g Bunch of carrots
- 1/2 bunch chives

preparation

60 minutes

1 poultry scissors. Wash the chicken pieces, pat dry and season with salt and coarse pepper. Preheat the oven (electric stove: 200 ° C / convection: 180 ° C / gas: see manufacturer).
2 Heat the oil in a roaster or an ovenproof pan. Fry the meat all around until golden brown, remove. Sweat the curry paste and 1 teaspoon of curry powder in the hot frying fat, deglaze with coconut milk. Bring to the boil, reduce a little and season with salt, pepper and lime juice. Add meat again. Braise in a hot oven for about 35 minutes. Mix the honey and 1 teaspoon of cumin, brush the meat with it approx. 10 minutes before the end of the roasting time.

3   In the meantime, peel the carrots, leaving some green on them. Wash the carrots and cut in half lengthways. Cook in boiling salted water for about 5 minutes until al dente. Take the chicken out of the oven. Drain the carrots and add to the finished chicken.

4   Wash the chives or carrot leaves as desired, shake dry, cut into small pieces and sprinkle over them. Serve the honey-curry chicken. If you don't want to eat low-carbohydrates, bread is enough.

Macros Nutritional info

1 portion approx:

- 350 kcal
- 31 g protein
- 19 g fat
- 12 g of carbohydrates

Potato and broccoli soup for the mini budget

Ingredients For 4 persons

- onion
- 500 g broccoli
- 500 g Potatoes
- 1 tbsp butter
- 2 tbsp Vegetable broth (instant)
- 250 g Frozen peas
- Salt pepper
- 3 tbsp whole almonds
- 1/2 bunch flat leaf parsley
- tbsp Whipped cream

preparation

40 minutes

1. Peel and dice the onion. Clean and wash broccoli and cut into florets. Peel and wash broccoli stalk and potatoes and roughly dice, except for 1 potato. Heat 2 tbsp butter in a saucepan. Sauté the onion, potatoes and stalk in it. Pour in 1 1⁄2 l of water, bring to the boil and stir in the stock. Simmer for about 15 minutes. Cook broccoli after approx. 8 minutes, frozen peas after approx. 10 minutes.
2. Cut the remaining potato into thin slices. Fry in 1 tablespoon of hot butter for about 10 minutes. Season with salt and pepper.

3   Chop the almonds. Wash parsley, shake dry and chop. Puree the soup very finely. Season to taste with salt and pepper. Serve with cream, almonds and parsley. Serve with potato slices.

Macros Nutritional info

1 portion approx:

- 300 kcal
- 12 g protein
- 13 g fat
- 31 g of carbohydrates

Powerful oven shakshuka

Ingredients For 4 persons

- 1 can (s) (425 ml each) Kidney beans
- 1 can (s) (425 ml each) giant white beans
- 100 g Baby spinach
- 150 g Cherry tomatoes
- 300 g Mushrooms
- 1 onion
- 1 clove of garlic
- 2 tbsp olive oil
- Salt, pepper, sugar
- can (s) (425 ml each) chunky tomatoes
- 4th Eggs (size M)
- 150 g Feta

preparation

45 minutes

1   Rinse the beans in the sieve and let them drain. Sort the spinach, wash and spin dry. Wash tomatoes, cut in half. Clean the mushrooms, wash them if necessary and cut them into quarters. Peel the onion and garlic, chop both. Preheat the oven (electric stove: 180 ° C / convection: 160 ° C / gas: see manufacturer).

2   Heat oil in a large pan. Fry the mushrooms, onion and garlic vigorously. Season with salt and pepper. Deglaze with chunky tomatoes and 100 ml of water. Bring to the boil and simmer for about 5 minutes. Season well with salt, pepper and sugar. Stir in 3⁄4 spinach, cherry tomatoes and beans, continue cooking for approx. 2 minutes.

3   Put everything in a baking dish (approx. 20 x 30 cm). Using a trowel or spoon, press in a hollow one after the other and beat 1 egg into each hollow. Cook in the hot oven for 6–8 minutes, until the eggs are set. Meanwhile, crumble the feta. Take out Shakshuka. Sprinkle with the rest of the spinach and feta.

Macros Nutritional info

1 portion approx:

- 330 kcal
- 24 g protein
- 15 g fat
- 24 g of carbohydrates

Cauliflower and lentil pan

Ingredients For 4 persons

- Head of cauliflower (approx. 900 g)
- 250 g Carrots
- 80 g dried dates
- 3 tbsp oil
- 200 g Red lenses
- 1 tsp Curry powder
- 2 tsp lactose-free instant vegetable broth
- stem (s) coriander
- 200 g lactose-free yogurt
- 1 tsp food starch
- salt
- pepper

preparation

25 minutes

1   Clean and wash the cauliflower and cut into small florets. Clean and peel the carrots, halve lengthways and cut into pieces. Halve the dates lengthways and cut into slices

2   Heat oil in a large pan. Fry the cauliflower and carrots in it. Add lentils and dates, fry briefly, sprinkle with curry. Pour in 500 ml of water, bring to the boil, stir in the stock

and simmer over a medium heat for about 10 minutes, stirring occasionally

3   Wash the coriander, pat dry, pluck the leaves. Mix 150 g of yoghurt with starch. Stir the yoghurt into the lentils, season with salt and pepper. Place the rest of the yogurt as a blob on the lentil pan, sprinkle with coriander greens. Indian flatbread tastes good with it

Macros Nutritional info

1-person approx.:

- 320 kcal1340 kJ
- 17 g protein
- 6 g fat
- 45 g of carbohydrates

Quick noodles with broccoli in cream cheese sauce

Ingredients For 4 persons

- 300 g Carrots
- 750 g broccoli
- onion
- 1 tbsp oil
- 200 g Orecchiette pasta
- 1 l Vegetable broth
- pepper
- salt
- sugar
- 75 g sliced cooked ham
- 1/2 bunch chives
- 150 g low-fat herbal cream cheese (8% fat)
- 1 tsp food starch

preparation

30 minutes

1 Clean and peel the carrots, halve lengthways and cut into slices. Clean and wash broccoli and cut into small florets. Peel the stem and cut into slices. Peel onion and chop finely. Heat the oil in a saucepan, sauté the carrots and onions in it.

2 Add the pasta and pour in the broth. Season with pepper, salt and sugar, simmer for about 12 minutes. After about 5 minutes of cooking, add the broccoli.

3   Cut ham into strips. Wash the chives, shake dry and cut into rolls. Stir the cream cheese into the pasta, bring to the boil. Season everything again to taste. Mix the starch with a little water until smooth, thicken the sauce with it.

4   Serve the pasta sprinkled with ham and chives.

Macros Nutritional info

1 portion approx:

- 340 kcal1420 kJ
- 19 g protein
- 7 g fat
- 47 g of carbohydrates

Couscous-style cauliflower with yogurt

Ingredients For 4 persons

- 1 Head of cauliflower
- 1 Kohlrabi with green
- Red onions
- Garlic cloves
- 1 federal government parsley
- 1 can (s) (425 ml) Chickpeas
- 60 ml orange juice
- 2 tbsp Fruit vinegar
- 1 tbsp honey
- tbsp olive oil
- Salt pepper
- Cayenne pepper
- 100 g more greek
- Cream yogurt

preparation

20 minutes

1. For the couscous, wash and drain cauliflower. Roughly grate the cabbage around the stalk into a large bowl.
2. Clean the kohlrabi, putting the heart leaves aside. Peel the kohlrabi and cut into sticks. Peel the onions and cut into thin wedges. Peel garlic and chop finely. Wash the parsley and kohlrabi leaves, shake dry and roughly chop.

3   Rinse the chickpeas in a colander with cold water and drain them.
4   For the marinade, mix together orange juice, vinegar and honey. Beat in 4 tablespoons of oil. Season well with salt, pepper and cayenne pepper.
5   Heat 2 tablespoons of oil in a large pan. Fry the onions, kohlrabi, chickpeas and garlic for about 3 minutes while turning. Season with salt and pepper. Mix with the marinade, parsley and kohlrabi leaves into the cauliflower.
6   Season to taste with salt and pepper. Serve with yogurt.

Macros Nutritional info

1-person approx:

- 350 kcal
- 1 g protein
- 22 g fat
- 24 g of carbohydrates

Carrot and fish ragout with chili

Ingredients For 4 persons

- 1 onion
- Chilli pepper
- 400 g Carrots
- 1 federal government Spring onions
- 600 g Pollack fillet
- 3 tbsp oil
- salt
- pepper
- Curry powder
- 1 tsp Vegetable broth (instant)
- tsp food starch

preparation

30 minutes

1 Peel and dice the onion. Cut the chilli open, remove the seeds, wash and chop. Peel or clean the carrots and spring onions, wash and cut into small pieces.
2 Rinse the fish, pat dry, chop roughly. Fry in hot oil, season with salt and pepper, remove. Sauté the prepared ingredients and 2 teaspoons of curry in the frying fat. Add 400 ml of water and stock, bring to the boil and simmer for about 10 minutes.

3   Mix starch with 2 tablespoons of water, bind the curry with it. Heat the fish in it. In addition: rice.

Macros Nutritional info

1-person approx:

- 220 kcal
- 29 g protein
- 6 g fat
- 11 g of carbohydrates

Pumpkin ratatouille

Ingredients For 4 persons

- 1/2 Hokkaido pumpkin (approx. 500 g each)
- Bell peppers (red and yellow)
- Shallots
- 3 tbsp oil
- 2 tbsp light balsamic vinegar
- 1 can (s) (425 ml each) Cherry tomatoes
- 1 Star anise
- Salt, pepper, sugar
- stem / s Thyme and oregano

preparation

40 minutes

1   Clean and wash the pumpkin and peppers. Cut the vegetables into small pieces. Peel
    and finely dice shallots. Heat the oil in a large saucepan, fry the shallots in it for about 1
    minute. Add the pumpkin and bell pepper. Fry for about 5 minutes, stirring constantly.
2   Deglaze with vinegar. Add tomatoes with juice, anise and 100 ml of water. Bring to the
    boil, season with salt, pepper and sugar. Cover and simmer over low to medium heat for
    15–20 minutes.
3   Wash the herbs, shake dry and pluck the leaves off. Stir into the ratatouille, season with
    salt and pepper.

Macros Nutritional info

1 portion approx:

- 140 kcal
- 3 g protein
- 5 g of fat
- 18 g of carbohydrates

Asian rice soup

Ingredients For 1 person

- 25 g Basmati rice
- salt
- 1 (approx. 50 g) carrot
- 1/2 yellow pepper
- 50 g sugar snap
- 150 ml vegetable stock
- Soy sauce
- handle (s) coriander

preparation

15 minutes

1 Prepare rice in boiling salted water according to the instructions on the packet. Peel the carrot, cut in half and cut into fine sticks. Clean and wash the peppers and sugar snap peas and cut into fine strips. Drain the rice and drain well in the sieve

2 Bring the vegetable stock to the boil in a saucepan. Add the vegetables and cook for 3–4 minutes. Season with soy sauce. Wash the coriander, pluck the leaves and finely chop.

Pour rice and vegetable soup into a bowl, sprinkle with coriander. Garnish with sakura cress if you like

Macros Nutritional info

1-person approx:

- 140 kcal580 kJ
- 5 g protein
- 1 g fat
- 30 g of carbohydrates

Carrot noodles with creamy pea sauce

Ingredients For 4 persons

- 300 g frozen peas
- 500 g Carrots
- 1 onion
- 1 clove of garlic
- 4 tbsp Sunflower oil
- salt
- 3 tbsp Whole milk yogurt
- pepper
- 2 red chili peppers
- 25 g Pine nuts

preparation

30 minutes

1 Put the peas in a bowl. Roast pine nuts in a pan without fat, turning and remove.
2 Peel the carrots and cut into thin strips with a peeler. Peel the onion and cut into fine cubes. Peel garlic and chop finely. Heat oil in a pot. Sauté the onion and garlic in it for about 5 minutes. After about 2 minutes add the peas.
3 Cook the carrots in boiling salted water for 4–5 minutes. Take the pea mixture out of the pot except for 4 tablespoons, puree with the yogurt and 3 tablespoons carrot water.

Season the sauce with salt and pepper. Clean and wash the chilli and cut into fine rings. Drain the carrots in a sieve. Arrange the carrots and sauce on a plate. Sprinkle with the remaining peas, pine nuts and chilli.

Macros Nutritional info

1-person approx:

- 190 kcal790 kJ
- 7 g protein
- 10 g fat
- 17 g of carbohydrates

Onion Chicken with Tomatoes

Ingredients For 10 persons

- 1 kg Cherry tomatoes
- 500 g small onions
- Bunch / pots of basil
- 12 (approx. 1.8 kg) Chicken fillets
- salt
- pepper
- sugar
- 8-10 tbsp olive oil
- 1 tsp broth
- grated zest of 1–2 organic lemons

preparation

45 minutes

1. Wash tomatoes, cut in half or leave whole, depending on size. Peel the onions and cut into thick rings. Wash the basil, pluck the leaves and set some aside.
2. Wash the fillets, pat dry and season with salt and pepper. Heat the oil in the roaster. Fry the fillets for 2 minutes per side.
3. Sauté the onions in the hot frying fat. Briefly sauté the tomatoes. Season with a little sugar, salt and pepper. Add approx. 200 ml of water and stock, bring to the boil. Put the

fillets in and cook covered for about 10 minutes.

4   Mix in the basil and lemon zest. Season everything to taste and garnish with the rest of the basil.

Macros Nutritional info

1-person approx:

- 250 kcal
- 35 g protein
- 8 g of fat
- 9 g of carbohydrates

Mushroom pan with light aioli

Ingredients For 4 persons

- 2 tbsp light salad cream
- 4 tbsp milk
- Garlic cloves
- Salt pepper
- 750 g Mushrooms
- 500 g Oyster mushrooms
- 1 federal government Spring onions
- 3 tbsp olive oil
- 150 g Whole grain baguette

preparation

40 minutes

1   Mix the salad cream and milk. Peel the garlic, crush it finely and stir in. Season to taste with salt and pepper.
2   Clean the mushrooms, wash them if necessary. Cut smaller depending on the size. Clean and wash the spring onions and cut into rings.
3   Heat the oil one after the other in a coated pan. Fry the mushrooms in portions. Return all of the mushrooms to the pan. Fry the spring onions briefly. Season the mushroom pan with salt and pepper.
4   Serve with aioli. In addition: baguette.

Macros Nutritional info

1 portion approx:

- 240 kcal
- 12 g protein
- 8 g of fat
- 28 g of carbohydrates

Beguiling lentil soup "magic ginger"

Ingredients For 6 persons

- 1 Hokkaido pumpkin (approx. 1.2 kg each)
- Zucchini (approx. 250 g each)
- Onions
- Garlic cloves
- 1 piece (approx. 4 cm each) ginger
- 4 tbsp oil
- 300 g yellow lentils (alternatively red lentils)
- Curry powder, salt, pepper
- 2 tbsp Agave syrup
- 2 tsp Vegetable broth (instant)
- Bay leaves
- 400 g Cherry tomatoes
- 1 pomegranate
- Avocados
- 2 Limes
- 150 g Greek cream yogurt

preparation

50 minutes

1. Wash the pumpkin, cut in half, remove the seeds and soft fibers. Cut the pumpkin into cubes. Wash, clean and dice the zucchini. Peel and finely dice onions, garlic and ginger.
2. Heat the oil in a large saucepan. Sauté onions, garlic and ginger in it. Add the pumpkin and zucchini, fry for about 5 minutes. Rinse, drain and add the lentils. Dust with 1 tbsp curry and sweat. Pour in 1.4 l of water and agave syrup, bring to the boil. Stir in the vegetable stock, add the bay leaf. Season with salt and pepper. Cover and simmer for about 20 minutes.
3. Wash and quarter the cherry tomatoes. Halve the pomegranate and remove the seeds. Halve and core the avocados. Remove the pulp from the skin with a tablespoon and cut into small pieces. Drizzle with half of the lime juice.
4. Puree some of the soup as desired. Heat the tomatoes in the soup. Season to taste with salt, pepper and the rest of the lime juice. Stir in yogurt (do not boil anymore!). Serve with avocado pieces and pomegranate seeds.

Macros Nutritional info

1 portion approx:

- 250 kcal
- 13 g protein
- 10 g fat
- 28 g of carbohydrates

Zucchini noodles with prawns

Ingredients For 4 persons

- 500 g frozen raw shrimp (headless, in shell)
- 2 yellow and green zucchinis (approx. 300 g each)
- 2 Garlic cloves
- 2 Organic lemons
- salt
- pepper
- 1 tbsp oil
- 4 stem (s) parsley

preparation

20 minutes

1 Put the prawns in a colander and let thaw for about 1 hour. Peel the prawns, remove the intestines, wash and pat dry. Wash zucchini, rub dry and peel into strips with a julienne peeler.

2 Peel and finely dice the garlic. Wash 1 lemon and rub dry. Rip off the shell. Halve the lemon and squeeze out the juice. Wash the parsley, shake dry and pluck the leaves from the stems.

3 Season the prawns with salt and pepper, heat the oil in a pan. Fry the prawns in it, turning, for about 5 minutes. Remove and add zucchini noodles to the pan. Fry for about

2 minutes, turning, season with salt and pepper.

4   Add the prawns, lemon zest and juice, simmer for about 2 minutes. Wash the rest of the lemon, rub dry and cut into thin wedges. Mix the parsley into the zucchini noodles and serve.

5   Garnish with lemon wedges.

Macros Nutritional info

1-person approx:

- 160 kcal670 kJ
- 23 g protein
- 5 g of fat
- 6 g of carbohydrates

Tin vegetables with herb curd cream

Ingredients For 4 persons

- 600 g Potatoes (mainly waxy)
- 1/2 (approx. 500 g) Hokkaido pumpkin
- 2 (approx. 300 g) small zucchini
- Sprigs of rosemary
- salt
- pepper
- 2 tbsp + 2 teaspoons of olive oil
- 250 g red and yellow cherry tomatoes
- 250 g medium sized white mushrooms
- 1 federal government chives
- 1 federal government parsley
- 500 g lowfat quark
- 100 ml low-fat milk (1.5% fat)
- 4-5 tbsp Mineral water

preparation

75 minutes

1 Wash, peel and quarter the potatoes and place in cold water. Remove the seeds from the pumpkin, cut the pumpkin into wedges. Wash the zucchini, pat dry and cut into thick slices. Wash the rosemary and chop it roughly into pieces

2   Drain the potatoes and place in a large bowl with the pumpkin wedges, zucchini and rosemary. Season with salt and pepper, sprinkle with 2 tablespoons of olive oil and mix everything well.

3   Brush a drip pan of the oven (33 x 39 cm) with 1 teaspoon of oil. Spread the vegetables on top and fry in the preheated oven (electric stove: 200 ° C / convection: 175 ° C / gas: see manufacturer) for about 45 minutes

4   Wash and drain the cherry tomatoes. Clean the mushrooms. Put the tomatoes and mushrooms in the still slightly oily bowl, season with salt and pepper, add 1 teaspoon of oil and mix well. After 20-25 minutes, add to the remaining vegetables in the drip pan, turning the vegetables on the drip pan if necessary

5   Wash the chives and parsley and shake dry. Cut the chives into fine rolls, chop the parsley. Mix the quark, milk and mineral water together until creamy. Stir in the herbs, except for something to sprinkle, and season with salt and pepper. Serve the herb quark cream with the sheet vegetables

Macros Nutritional info

1-person approx:

- 320 kcal1340 kJ
- 25 g protein
- 9 g fat
- 32 g of carbohydrates

Cloud eggs

Ingredients For 4 persons

- Parchment paper
- 4th Eggs (size M)
- 1 tbsp grated parmesan or vegetarian hard cheese
- pepper

preparation

15 minutes

1. Preheat the oven for 4 people (electric stove: 200 ° C / convection: 180 ° C / gas: see manufacturer). Line a baking sheet with parchment paper. Separate 4 eggs (size M), put the egg yolks aside in the shell halves (e.g., in the egg box). Beat the egg whites until stiff. Fold in 1 tablespoon of grated parmesan. Spread the egg whites in 4 piles on the tray. Press a teaspoon into the center. Bake in the hot oven for about 6 minutes. Let the egg yolks slide into the hollows and bake for another 3 minutes. Season with pepper.
2. Also tastes good sprinkled with herbs on toasted bread with crispy bacon.

Macros Nutritional info

1 portion approx:

- 95 kcal
- 8 g protein
- 6 g fat

- 1 g of carbohydrates

Whole wheat bread with cream cheese, sprouts and sun-dried tomatoes

Ingredients For 4 persons

- 100 g Lentil sprouts
- 1/2 glass (225 g each) sun-dried tomatoes, pickled in oil
- slices Whole grain bread (approx. 45 g each)
- 100 g Double cream cream cheese

preparation

10 mins

1   Put the sprouts in a colander, rinse and drain. Drain the tomatoes and roughly chop them.
2   Brush the bread slices with cream cheese, spread the tomatoes and sprouts on top.

Macros Nutritional info

1-person approx:

- 220 kcal920 kJ
- 6 g protein
- 11 g fat

- 24 g of carbohydrates

Ham toast with cress

Ingredients For 1 person

- 1 slice Whole grain toast bread
- 1 Lettuce leaf
- 50 g Buttermilk Quark
- salt
- colored pepper
- 25 g cooked ham in wafer-thin slices
- 1/4 Bed of cress

preparation

10 mins

1. Toast the bread until golden brown in the toaster, allow to cool. Wash the lettuce, pat dry. Season the quark with salt and pepper. Brush the bread slice with it. Top with salad and ham. Cut the cress from the bed, sprinkle over it.
2. Sprinkle with pepper.

Macros Nutritional info

1-person approx:

- 130 kcal540 kJ
- 14 g protein
- 2 g of fat

- 15 g of carbohydrates

Berry crispy quark

Ingredients For 1 person

- 1 tsp Almond flakes
- 75 g mixed berries (e.g. raspberries, blueberries, blackberries)
- 1/2 untreated lemon
- 150 g lowfat quark
- 5-6 tbsp Mineral water
- 1 tsp Agave syrup
- 1/2 slice Wholegrain crispbread

preparation

15 minutes

1   Roast the almonds in a pan without fat, remove them and let them cool
2   Sort the berries, wash them if necessary and let them drain. Wash the lemon with hot water, rub dry, finely grate the peel. Squeeze the lemon. Mix the quark, mineral water, lemon zest, 1–2 tablespoons lemon juice and agave syrup

3   Crumble the crispbread. Arrange the quark and berries in a bowl, sprinkle with almonds and crumbled crisps

Macros Nutritional info

1-person approx:

- 230 kcal960 kJ
- 23 g protein
- 5 g of fat
- 23 g of carbohydrates

CPSIA information can be obtained
at www.ICGtesting.com
Printed in the USA
BVHW052135250621
610374BV00013B/2097

9 781803 077706